A Cat In Quarantine

Written and Illustrated
By
Joanne G. Garcia

To all the cats who have filled our hearts
with joy and have had to put up with us.

A Cat In Quarantine by Joanne G. Garcia
Story and Illustrations © 2020 by Joanne G. Garcia

ISBN-13: 978-0-578-73743-0

2020

joannegarcia.myportfolio.com

You are about to hear a story as told by a cat. It is about how I got through the 2020 quarantine, due to this thing called COVID-19.

My humans are kind and work during the day. While they are out, I have all day to play.

I am a good cat who likes to help out, keeping the floor dry from that drippy drip spout.

I keep an eye on the garden from indoors, of course. My humans must appreciate it and leave me this cushion, which they call a purse.

Sometimes a few things may be out of place. I will rearrange them and give them some space.

When it comes to my naptime, my choices are many. A couch, a chair, or a bed are more than plenty.

Life as I knew it was about to change. Suddenly my humans were home all day, and that's when things got strange.

It was all over the news, and this "shelter in place" was rattling their nerves. They had to stay home to flatten the curve.

They washed their hands before any task.
When they stepped outside they even wore
a mask.

They began to clean and mess up my things.
They even found my collection of rings.

"Off the table!" I was told and had to get off the purse. Even drinking from the drippy spout made things even worse.

Trying to cope as best as I could, I even let them pet me more than I should.

Even naptime became quite a chore. All my favorite spots were taken except for the floor.

I got along with my humans, even though it was rough. I learned it is best to love and help one another more when times get tough.

I love my family, and they love me.
That is why we are quite the team during uncertanties, like this 2020 quarantine.

Things will get better all in due time, and when this is all over...the house will once again be mine!

About the cat:
This story is about a cat named Sky.
When left alone, he loves to sit on top of tables and knock things over counters. During the pandemic of 2020, he had to adapt to his humans being home and occupying his space. Sky learned to adapt to his new surroundings and face any challenge that comes his way.

About the author:
Joanne G. Garcia is an artist with a BFA in Animation and Entertainment Art from CSUF. She is the author and illustrator of "Girafficorns" and has worked in film, television, games, and product design.

Website: joannegarcia.myportfolio.com
Facebook & Instagram: fiercefantasydesigns

www.ingramcontent.com/pod-product-compliance
Lightning Source LLC
Chambersburg PA
CBHW041550040426
42447CB00002B/121